A Heart Worth Breaking

A Heart Worth Breaking

Poems by

Lindsay Evelyn Hamilton

Cover design by Shay Culligan
Cover image by Kevin Pastor on Unsplash
Author photo by Janet L. DeMaio

ISBN: 978-1-63980-723-9

Kelsay Books
502 South 1040 East, A-119
American Fork, Utah 84003
Kelsaybooks.com

for the ones who will know who they are when they read this

Acknowledgments

My greatest thanks is for my son, Sean, who is my heart and soul, my reason for writing and breathing. He has worked with me to create a life in which we both can do what we love. I'd also like to thank my sister Laura, a published poet herself, for sharing her talent with me and unofficially editing my whole life. My mother, too, has always accepted me for the eccentric person I am and encouraged me to make a life from what I love to do. Which is to write, of course.

Contents

The River

Much of love is lost in translation. It is lost
to the wind when it scatters your words
through the dust coughed up
by golden-green miles
Or the sayings time steals from our lips when they are not pressed
together,
soft as the inside
of a splayed-open fruit.

I used to fear the ache time carved in my soul
as it carried us further
down the stream of a life apart.
But now I know:
Love is not lost in the vicious things we said
when our oneness was pulled at the seams by the long agony of
miles;
nor was it lost in the soulful words we swallowed
which now salt the back of our throats.

Real love is never lost
but flows through each parted lover
like a river or a stream.
More steadfast even than the earth
that grew me, water is unending;
it transcends time and space,
life and death.

Love in its purest form is a woman made of water
who flows to me without fear
and moves through me, yes,
like a river or a stream.
She is lost not in translation nor
the years that go by
in a city that won't sleep
and a golden-green town that won't wake.

Love is an open window. Through it
I can see the sun burst through
your open face in a moment of joy
that crept upon us too late-
The dream was over.
Love is the burning-hot core of that sun,
sizzling to my touch when no one was looking.

Nothing ends that has always been
and so through the rush of time and space
I will return, not ebb away.
Wait for me where hello kissed goodbye
and you left,
taking with you the sky and the sea and the sand.
I know the river still runs through us.

We Are

Rage lights the ember of your soul
and hate, too, is an enduring warmth,
stretching as madly as passion across miles.
It lights you as a candle does a room
clearing the sage-burnt air,
but on the other side of that tender wick,
I melt into love.

I am the keeper of sacred things,
the ocean of grief that cannot contain
love's overflow.
I am the wave you want to swallow down
like whiskey, but it bubbles up
from darkest pitch and becomes you.

What are we if not the white-hot,
fearful flame of soul
love burns us down to?
I hold you inside me
as the candle does ambient light,
wrapping silk around your night-dark skin.
This mad, starving grief for the one
who shored up the sea of my soul
is not stronger than the lover
who burns against it.

Still, love blisters through my days
like holiness through ether,
the redeeming sun through a thin-veiled sky.
I want to pick up the torch of my strength
and take up Plath's refrain: *I am, I am, I am.*
But my heart says, *We are.*

If It Is Love

Love, if it is love, lends itself
to extremes. I cannot be felt and taken back if it won't fit—
You have to wear it in like an old beloved shoe.
You want to reel it back, but the everlasting thread extends
itself like a ribbon of gold
from one heart to its other. It leads to the soul,
which flows out like a river of joy or sorrow
depending on the turn of her dime.

A storm may sweep in to gather the ripeness
that was harvested from your heart
when love was in full bloom,
petals peeled back to reveal the red rose core-
But now the winter has come.

Maybe you picked the ripest one and still got the seed.
Maybe the gem of your soul was unearthed
the light shining through the rough of it,
but the sight was not miracle enough to hold love's gaze-
or it was too much of one,
too hot in a love's hands
and so it slipped from them,
Love, if it is love, is still not larger than life's frailty.

The force of your nature is not to be reckoned with;
in a single act of defiance,
you might tear the earth from its roots.
But with fragile glass windows for eyes,
You stare into the ocean-depth of my soul
and it spills from me like a river.

Some of us are too much for hands to hold;
we bubble over like lava
or slip through the cracks in our armor.
I never minded; your overflow is sacred to me.
I want to take it into my mouth like a communion. It bursts
inside me, a joy.

If I must crash and burn a thousand times, I will
So long as it is into you and we feed the flames of our fire
with more fire.

The Longest Goodbye

There is such a thing as loving too much.
When I look at you, my heart full to bursting,
and I cannot staunch the overflow,
I think: For what you have lost
I cannot make up.
But I can surround you so fully that it insulates you
as snow softens the dead of winter,
as soil hugs the root of rose
so that it flowers into fullness once a year.

Life is the longest goodbye
but we can stretch it at the worn seams,
draw it out over thirty more years
of one more kiss before the train takes me home.
One more look through the windows of your eyes
into the ocean-depth of love
before the tides of time wash me back onto shore,
apart.

From the harvest of your heart,
open as a child's on Christmas,
I can harvest a life. We don't need the raw materials
with which to build a house
or a dwelling. Anywhere, I can look into those windows for eyes
and be home.

The Path of Least Resistance

The purest breath of winter
was the one you stole from me
without meaning to steal my breath at all;
like some prehistoric truth of what a man should be
before the nature of men was lost,
you stood sentinel in a field of snow
falling softly.

What magic has slipped through my fingertips
you caught in an iron fist;
what was unknown to me you learned
from letting go of all I hunt down to the bone.

The path of least resistance
is not nearly so mountainous as my love
looming larger than life can be;
your magic is in such simple majesties
as the delicate pulse at the throat
of hunted prey that still hunts
the throb of light beneath what is frozen.
There is no wilder territory
than my heart laid bare by those hunter's hands.

Though I'll deny it till the day I die
I am a dreamer of dreams to life
and I dreamed you smoothed over my path
as snow does rocky terrains.

If the thorned past grew too sharply
through the earth, then you are
the hope of a calm aftermath,
a comfort I craved without knowing
that comfort could be cold
and then melt like honey into ease.

A truer word for ease is submission
but it rests like a prayer on silenced lips
from which the purest breath was stolen.

You stole it without meaning
to steal my breath at all;
still I want to choke your softness in a tighter fist
than the one that squeezed mine from me.
Though the walls tremble in heat
and ice melts, I refuse to chase the light in our shadow
further than it carries itself
through wild territories.

The grim bearer of truths,
you dealt the harshest of all:
I cannot have what I want by default
of wanting it, cannot love the devil out of an angel
who has fallen so far from the mountain
looming larger than life can be.

They say love is not setting someone on fire
to see if they burn for you,
but I do, and no calm hand
tempers the flames.

She Loves Me Not

I've never plucked a petal
off a rose in bloom
from sacred roots and said you love me;
if I do, our gentleness might take its fiery leave of me
and I, flushed as that summer rose,
will be soft as a wound
with thorns stuck in it.

I am stronger than that,
stronger still than the conquered self who is now
trembling like the sea behind a dam.
In the shattered window of my mind
your soul, a bird in hand, has flown away,
trading roots for freedom.

Yet here you are,
a vision in white flowering through dreams,
sparked back to waking life
and freer, too, than a far-flung dove
across many skies.

I Told No One

Spring held me softly in its favor
and I told no one
of the secret, fevered spaces we slipped into
like honeyed light through cracked ice.
My world when it ended began again
with a cleaner slate than the sky,
and I told no one.

You are not the riotous spring
which flowers and then fades,
but the gentle, throbbing light
that melts glaciers over years,
over centuries.

When the faces of dandelions
open like tiny suns and lean toward the sky,
you are as firmly rooted in yourself
as a tall willow weeping for bygones.
I wept silently, too, for your losses
and told no one.

The shimmering soft spot in my heart
where you are most alive
does not burst open like the sun
In June; it rather steeps itself in silence
Waiting, as ever, to begin again.

The Tapestry

Today I take my fullness of heart
and do not close its blistered valve;
from these two hands like empty cups
I give it to the world,
an offering. An opening I long to receive
as a child of God would a communion.

Love, like art, is nothing if not melded from scratch
into tangibility; and so I paint it
onto the endless blank canvas of the sky
in the brilliant hope that you will open those windows for eyes
and see us as I do:

A tapestry stitched thinly together by God.
Like spun gold from ether
unwinding at the seams we did not tie
we can be free as the wind and still be one.

There is room to be like water
and flow out from behind a dam;
there is courage enough in my heart
to sink and to swim again.
The tidal wave comes
and I am an ocean of you and me.

Come, and be as true as love
when it flowers into fullness,
a crimson rose not unlike your mouth
when it is tender around my name.

Begin Again

Silence is not my first language
but it flows through your veins
like peace does rivers, and stops for nothing,
not even the thousand deaths that wither me.

I stand at the clean slate of a river
and am held at your strong arm's length,
but not forever; the calm surface splinters
and you slip into the cracks
of my suffering. Not to worry:
You are still the stark winter's white,
pure as the driven snow
and too fully your own to ever be mine.

But where others drowned
you shored up the sea of my soul
and that, I suppose,
is a good enough reason as any to love you.
Another: your stillness that steeps me
in my own, and reminds me that
the world, when it ends, can begin again.

The Harvest

In autumn you fall around me:
a bluster of leaves
in mad yellows curled like fire at the edges,
in rustic, tumbling reds
with soft golden underbellies.

You varied shades of bloom are not forgotten
but gathered in my heart,
a harvest growing wildly out of hands.

Should your vibrancy pulse deeply
through hallowed nerves
and not come back to me,
I will be stripped of all that melts
into meaning from ruin.

Heart of the Sea

To the rough and tumble edge of love
I wander, and each time I am sure
I will be steeped at length
in the heart of the sea,
in the churning depth of emotion
from which your soul springs.

And each time
there is only the tide crashing over me,
your salt tears in my throat
and the distant clamor of feet on dry land.

Who but a false God can say
which hand of time turns the tides,
which one of us gets to recede
While the other clamors onto dry land?

From my soul a cavern of loss is carved
by the sharp knife of your tongue;
I want to crumple the force of your nature
and toss it to the wind.
I want to slice you open like a summer fruit
splayed to its inner ripe parts
and taste and feed and grow.

The Travelers

A world between two travelers
is woven from a tapestry of souvenirs,
small things lifted and not returned:
The borrowed warmth of your down jacket
when the winter months have stripped me to the bone
And yes, your arms fast around me
The long ambience of your journey toward my light
and the end of the tunnel
and you thought it was the sun spilling gently from ether,
the soft reprieve of morning after a dark night of the soul
When in truth it was fire,
which does not take kindly to gentility.

To mold a man into a god
is to fell him slowly from grace,
this I know.
If I could slip backward through time
and find your face open like the sun
when it drinks me in,
I would graciously allow your human frailty
to melt into my cracks,
letting the light into all the spaces
where violence has splintered me apart
and growth would stretch sinuously through my muscles,
making them long and limber.

Time will not date the afterglow of ecstasy;
it still hatches from my cold heart
the way light hatches from a wintry sun
though you are timeworn and heavily laden with the past.
Sadness has not spoiled the joy of togetherness,
nor curdled it like old milk into something unpleasant.
It still glows like the subtle lights on the tree we strung,
among birds, small wings of life fluttering in our scrunched faces
Reminding us that innocence can be lost
and then found again.
That life can be extinguished and then born again.

Must we bottle joy like a firefly in a child's glass jar
Or might it glow freely in the dark,
existing for its own sake?
It is all or it is nothing; that is who you are,
and I succumb to your iron will.
I could write you the world, or at least ours,
but in the end the words fall flat on my tongue.
The only thing left:
to show you it is not nothing, but all.

Homesick

They say the city never sleeps
but nor does the wilderness of love
that waits for us to shed our skin
of otherness and be one.
Your wildness, once tight in a bud,
is now in hot, volcanic bloom
and will stay open
until night closes the petals of your eyes
and mourning comes.

They told me to go home
but what of homes we make
away from those we've built like walls
around our hearts and outgrown?
What of the tidal loves that won't be stemmed
by safer, nearer shores?

I once stretched out goodbyes like miles
tautly as honeyed strands over hives,
but from time I've learned a trick:
If I tuck you into myself, you are everywhere.
The gold-tinged spring holds your lilac scent
like breath and exhales wind.

Half-lives orbit the sun of your soul
that sizzles like a fried egg in a pan,
burning me into it.
Home is the two-bit stove
where you slaved hotly over
what little we had,
making a meal of such raw, vivacious hunger.

Other Things

It's a fever breaking in the night
when you thought it would not go gently
But the room was warmer with us both in it, loosening
my bones until they were slack with the ease of newness.

Stagnation is an empty room before it fills with danger
But instead of death, you walked through the door
letting in with you the faint glow of hope, of otherness.
For an eternity I craved the sameness of a twin,
my counterpart. But your difference
struck like lightning, cleaved the tepid clouds
and light broke through again.

It is an insulation from a force that might have wrecked me
Had it not been the right place and time for you
to notice the lightness of the air around me
despite the cement-heaviness that pulled me to the earth
while you floated in your own electric sky
A world unto yourself, and the others
orbited around you like dutiful moons.
A figment of your own wild imaginings,
Drawn to life by your own rules like a God.
Who gave you the right?

My face was drawn tightly into itself
but yours was open like the sun
on a sweeter day in my life.

Perhaps if I'd not been wearing that dress
or the lightning in your veins was less scattered
in the storm, I would not have been drawn
into the dark center
the stirrings of which moved me to tears
on the first day of September
when the world was wiped clean like a canvas,
and maybe the storm had passed.

My face is no longer drawn tightly into itself
like it was on the day we met.
But yours is no longer open like the sun
on a sweeter day in my memory.

The season turned and the world bloomed
but I was dying again
and you were busy doing other things.
Life is here and then it's gone;
there is nothing new about me.
Yet my pain always seems to shock me
like the first wound of a newborn soul
when the world dashes its daringness to dream.

What is my need to cut sharply into comfort,
rendering it cold?
I wanted to hurt you before you hurt me
and then maybe you could have a swing or two,
and we could shrug it off like rough-and-tumble children.
But you were busy doing other things.

Stronger Still

Do not push heavily through my veins,
molten like lava and heedless of my soft skin.
I know it's been what you call a fortnight
and there's a shaky held breath between us,
slight enough to swallow us whole.
But urgency borders on the edge of madness
and I do not want to smolder like a long-lost lover
at the shore of your stemmed tide,
the light on your face caught in my raw throat.
I cannot swallow the lump of it.

For Christmas you sent me your words;
they arrived home instead of you
like postcards on my doorstep.
If a season's greeting is all you'll be
I am still gifted beyond luck.
Beyond rhyme, beyond reason.
Even when you're gone you light me from the inside out,
lift the melancholy from the bed of my bones.
Did I ever tell you that? If so,
then not nearly enough and quite possibly under my breath.
And so the last favor I'll ask is one too many,
but you are kind, so you'll grant it to me anyway:
Hold me at an ambient distance,
a strong arm's length
and the winter will not cut me to the bone.

Before your strength was gentled in my wake
I had not known it could melt like butter into submission
Mine and yours, though I wore it like your favorite dress.
It clung to me like sunlight to a summer's day,
and so did you, for so long.

I stopped counting the hours lost
and started counting them as blessings:
The butterflies that swarmed your heart
when life was nearly hatched from our midst
The long steps you took toward my door,
Your feet eating up the miles as if nothing could go wrong
The childlike excitement that leapt like a flame
From you when your eyes lit on my face
A pounding of light into my body
until stars exploded in my vision
And then the reprieve of your stillness.

I absorbed you like the sun through my pores
on a winter's morning
and I grew healthier from it
Stronger against the storms.
I am stronger still.

Wildflower

You are all around me: a pale, holy sun burning
through the veil of heat
which separates heaven from this wreck of fire;
a grain of truth among rubble,
the deep stirring of a river
which to the naked eye
appears to have no churning depth.

Your pureness of heart
is mirrored by the bluest of skies,
seeded richly in the roots of sunlit fields:
fertile roots that, when watered,
give birth to love all over again.

From a tight bud, soft in its coil
year after year blooms the same wildflower.
Some loves will not be stemmed
by the humbleness of roots
or even by the end of loving.

We can pluck this feeling
and plant it where it grows
when seasons, like tides, change.
We can seed into our winter selves
and bloom again when the sunflowers
turn their open faces toward the light.

The Child Is Gone

A lover's rawness comes to me on the breeze . . .
It shivers hotly through parts of me hitherto unknown.
The air has never been sweeter on my tongue
than when he was sweet.
It is the work of an artist to tie nerve endings taut
only to sweep coolly over them
so that they sway like tall grass in the wind.

The sky is a clearer, wholesome blue in his wake;
it sears my soul with its purity.
Carefree as a child, he takes my hand in the light of day,
lavishes sweetness on me when no one is looking,
like a father sneaking cotton candy
behind a mother's back.
He shares in the sweetness of it all,
a spark in his wide eyes though they crinkle roughly with age . . .
A real lover is timeless.

My soul he peeled open like a flower,
petal by soft petal, until the core was exposed to light.
It bled its sweetness onto electric fingertips
and the world opened to me;
its endlessness swallowed me up.
Fear struck like white lightning
even as his hands calmed my depth into stasis
and love took the form of a slow-moving river until it froze.

Why would a lover want to be absolved of the life
he so naturally unveiled?
What rhyme or reason could there be
if not to kill it within oneself
and in turn negate childhood,
which believes that life is given and not created?

When a woman is dead to such a lover,
she wishes she truly were . . .
and after a while her wish is granted by time.
The nature of life is that it goes on,
but it will never be the same.

The lover, he washes back onto shore;
he ebbs and flows with the tides.
But the child is gone.

Without Thanks

She is spun not from silk but a tempest
gathering rapt souls into the hot center. They burn
blindly for her. Wrought from the grit and bearing
of a life that did not come easily,
she grants them less mercy than a fire
would a moth caught in its flame.

A woman splayed like an offering at the altar of her bed
Catches more honey from bees than vinegar.
Her sweetness she saves for those who are more contained
than her outsized heart
and are held safe there like children,
seen and not heard,
save for in the cloistered dark.

When dew parts the clouds and a storm hovers,
saving itself for later,
Summer drops heavily into the fullness of my lap
and the air, smelling ripely of peaches,
wraps itself sumptuously around her.

Heedless of my disdain
she blows smoke through bared teeth
and works the long day through
while the townspeople drift like waves onto lolling shores
burning their languor into a fried-egg sun.
In spite of myself, when the day is done,
I lift a cold glass of lemonade to her lips
and she drinks greedily from it, without thanks.

I Would Call It My Own

Time stops for no one. Not the girl
whose wildness erupts from a floret
into a bird of paradise
flying high into the great mouth of the sky,
or the world with its bared teeth.

Not the boy whose silence
flows through him like serenity does rivers,
and also stops for nothing:
Not even for the flower of a girl
nor the thousand deaths that wilt her.

Your silence is not native to me
but if I could, I would nestle quietly
into that soft, shimmering spot
where peace lives in your heart.
I would call it my own.

Where the Light Comes Through

When I think of you,
my soul does not burst open
like an overbright sun,
nor does it soar dangerously close
to that sun in a resplendent sky

but thaws. Do you know
the first subtle light of March,
the faint pulse of warmth
beneath the stillness of dead surfaces?
The finespun breaks in the ice
are where your light comes through.

The small fissures in my heart,
which was not cracked open all at once
this time, but kneaded softly
over treasured time,
are also where your light comes through.

My Son and Your Daughter

Out of the great, porous blue
comes the lightness of a child
with spring in her small bones.
She is the sun passing through
a quicksilver storm and not stopping,
not even for the hawk that swoops
down from the sky
and fells the day-old sparrow.

As sure as the sky is blue in my son's eyes
this world will break your heart
more deeply than God can mend it.
We spend this one and only life
chasing summers
through the long winter of it.

Like that fearful, fluttering bird
in the mouth of danger,
we imagine our only reprieve
comes in sunbursts, in fireworks;
forevers that flower open in a day,
like souls in the spring of love.

Unseeing that mostly, we live in the hives
of moments, in the cracks of our suffering,
glued together by my son and your daughter.

Lovechild

The trouble with intellectuals is that they deny their human nature
on the occasions that it simplifies them.
The human experience is neither an idea
Nor the lovechild of a fertile mind
and its daringness to dream.

Raw is the animal desire to be filled
and for new life to grow from that.
Men, like children, are nurtured within women
He seeks the highness of my love like a drug.
For him it is bathed in gold; it births things from the dark.

Oh, he knows not that the rawness of his heart,
soft when it swells, exhilarates me.
His soul takes the form of white light
and pulses through the sinews of strength
for he holds me safer than my mother did
in her broken, bloodied womb
when mankind was still waiting for me.

I wonder for the thousandth time
how any woman could press her fingers into those sinews of
strength
and still want someone else.

About the Author

Lindsay Evelyn Hamilton is a published poet and author of *Lily Whites of Steel* (Authorhouse, 2013). A copywriter by trade, she is also a screenwriter and TV and commercial actress. Lindsay has a bachelor's degree in communications with a focus in journalism from the University of Phoenix. After she earned her degree, her career took an unexpected turn when she was offered a job teaching screenwriting at a local acting school. Films she has co-written and starred in are currently streaming on several major platforms, including Tubi. Last but certainly not least, she is the mother of a brilliant teenage son.

www.ingramcontent.com/pod-product-compliance
Lightning Source LLC
Chambersburg PA
CBHW070907100426
42737CB00047B/2975